WOMEN
WIN THE VOTE

by Lee S. Justice

EDUCATORS PUBLISHING SERVICE
Cambridge and Toronto

© 2008 by School Specialty, Inc.

Series Authors: Kay Kovalevs and Alison Dewsbury
Commissioning Editors: Rachel Elliott, Tom Beran, Lynn Robbins, and Laura Woollett
Project managed by Rebecca Henson and Katherine Steward
Text by Lee S. Justice
Edited by Bronwyn Collie
Designed by Jenny Jones
Photographic research by Dan Nicholls

Making Connections® program developed by School Specialty, Inc. and by Pearson Australia (a division of Pearson Australia Group Pty Ltd).

ISBN 978 0 8388 3369 8

2013 2012 2011 2010
10 9 8 7 6 5 4 3 2

Printed in Dongguan City, Guang Dong Province, China, May 2010

Acknowledgements
The author and publisher would like to thank the following for permission to reproduce the copyright material in this book.

Photographs
Corbis, pp. 7, 10, 11, 14, 17, 21 (top), 22, 27, 28, 30; Getty Images, pp. 4, 12; Library of Congress Prints and Photographs Division Washington, pp. 5, 9, 13, 15, 21 (bottom), 23, 24, 25, 27, 29; Nebraska State Historical Society, p. 19; U.S Department of Interior, p. 18.

Every effort has been made to trace and acknowledge copyright. The author and publisher welcome any information from people who believe they own copyright material in this book.

Contents

CHAPTER 1

The Struggle Begins

Elizabeth was happy to take a break from her household chores. It was such a comfort to visit with an old friend! She and her friend Lucretia sipped tea and chatted. Three other women also joined them in the talk that summer day in 1848.

Elizabeth Cady Stanton and Lucretia Mott had first met eight years earlier. They had attended the World

Lucretia Mott (1793–1880) grew up with ideals of peace and equality. She spoke out against slavery and led women in anti-slavery organizations. Mott worked for women's rights and was known for her ability to stay calm when speaking to angry crowds. Women admired her for her ability to work and to care for her six children at the same time.

NOTMAN   BOSTON

Anti-Slavery Convention in London, England, with their husbands. Mott had planned to give a speech against slavery. But women were not allowed to speak at the meeting. They even had to sit apart from the men, behind a screen. Stanton and Mott had talked about how unfair that was.

Now, they talked again about women's place in the world. Stanton's voice rose with hope. Why shouldn't women be treated equally? Why not try to end the unfairness?

The group came up with a plan. They would have their own convention! They would invite people to share ideas about women's rights.

Elizabeth Cady Stanton holds one of her children.

The group wrote a document titled "The Declaration of Rights and Sentiments" to debate at the meeting. They used the Declaration of Independence as a model. The document listed "repeated injuries" against women. Women could not go to college. They had to give up ownership of their property to their husbands. And women were not allowed to vote in elections.

Below are excerpts from The Declaration of Rights and Sentiments (top) and the Declaration of Independence (bottom).

The Declaration of Rights and Sentiments, July 20, 1848: We hold these truths to be self-evident: that all men and women are created equal; that they are endowed by their Creator with certain inalienable rights; that among these are life, liberty, and the pursuit of happiness.

The Declaration of Independence, July 4, 1776: We hold these truths to be self-evident, that all Men are created equal, that they are endowed by their Creator with certain unalienable Rights, that among these are Life, Liberty, and the Pursuit of Happiness.

The only major difference between the two excerpts is the addition of the word "women."

Should women vote? Mott warned Stanton that the public would laugh at them for suggesting such a strange idea. But Stanton insisted on discussing voting rights at the meeting.

The convention began three days later, on July 19, 1848. It took place in Stanton's home town of Seneca Falls, New York. About 300 people attended. Mott's husband led the meeting because women rarely ran public meetings.

Frederick Douglass
(1818–1895)

The attendees debated each idea. When the question of voting rights came up, they could not agree. Then the great anti-slavery leader Frederick Douglass spoke. He said that the ability to vote was the most important right of all. It was needed to protect all other rights. The voting rights question passed.

The Seneca Falls Convention was the first major event in the struggle for women's voting rights in the United States. The women's suffrage movement had begun.

CHAPTER 2

Early Leaders

Most newspaper reports made fun of the call for women's rights. The idea of women voting or becoming lawyers was just too ridiculous. It was as silly as asking men to darn stockings or wash dishes!

Elizabeth Cady Stanton did not mind the ridicule. She wrote to Lucretia Mott that the reports were good for their cause. "When men and women think about a new question, the first step in progress is taken."

Stanton was right. Soon, other towns held women's rights conventions. The first national convention was held in 1850.

In 1851, Stanton met a woman who had come to Seneca Falls for an anti-slavery meeting. The woman was Susan B. Anthony. Stanton and Anthony became friends. They began to work together for women's rights. Stanton worked from home, where she continued to take care of her family. She wrote articles and pamphlets. She wrote speeches for Anthony to give at meetings.

Elizabeth Cady Stanton (1815–1902) was a famous writer and speaker. Her father once told her, "Oh my daughter, I wish you were a boy." After that, Stanton was determined to make him proud.

Stanton married her husband, Henry, in 1840. Stanton was not only interested in voting rights for women. Both she and Henry spoke out against slavery. After their wedding, they traveled to London, England to attend the World's Anti-Slavery Convention.

Susan B. Anthony's (1820–1906) parents always taught her that men and women were equal. At the age of seventeen, she worked as a teacher. She argued for equal pay with male teachers, who earned much more than women. Later, she became the most famous leader of the women's suffrage movement. Anthony traveled thousands of miles every year and gave hundreds of talks demanding women's voting rights. "There is no reason, no argument, nothing but prejudice, against our demand," she said.

Sojourner Truth (1797?–1883) was a powerful speaker. She had escaped slavery and went on to speak out against slavery and for women's suffrage. At a women's convention in Ohio, she listened to a minister say that women were not equal to men. She gave this speech as a response:

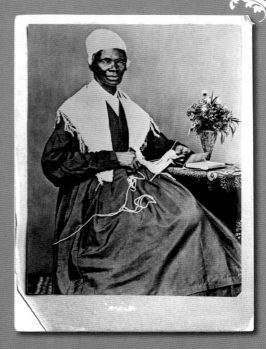

"That man over there says that women need to be helped into carriages, and lifted over ditches, and to have the best place everywhere. Nobody ever helps me into carriages, or over mud puddles, or gives me any best place. . . . And ain't I a woman? I have plowed, and planted, and gathered into barns, and no man could head me. And ain't I a woman? I could work as much and eat as much as a man—when I could get it—and bear the lash as well. And ain't I a woman?"
—SOJOURNER TRUTH, AKRON CONVENTION, MAY 1851

A National Effort

From 1861 to 1865, the nation split apart in war. Conflict over slavery was a main reason for the Civil War. Stanton and Anthony gathered signatures to support the end of slavery. They worked to amend, or change, the U.S. Constitution.

The Thirteenth Amendment of the Constitution ended slavery. Soon there was talk of two new amendments. These changes would protect the voting rights of citizens. Stanton and Anthony were thrilled. Women citizens would have the right to vote!

Elizabeth Cady Stanton (left) and Susan B. Anthony (right)

Supporters of women's voting rights, called suffragists, were soon terribly disappointed. The Fourteenth and Fifteenth Amendments protected the voting rights only of men. Half of all U.S. citizens still could not vote.

Stanton and Anthony did not give up. They organized suffragists' groups around the nation. They talked to lawmakers. They continued to speak out for suffrage. They would spend the rest of their lives in the effort.

The U.S. Constitution lays out the law of the land. An amendment is a change added to the end of the document. This is part of the Fifteenth Amendment: "The right of citizens of the United States to vote shall not be denied or abridged by the United States or by any State on account of race, color, or previous condition of servitude."

Article XV.

Section 1. The right of citizens of the United States to vote shall not be denied or abridged by the United States or by any State on account of race, color, or previous condition of servitude —

Section 2. The Congress shall have power to enforce this article by appropriate legislation —

Schuyler C. fax

Speaker of the House of Representatives.

CHAPTER 3

No Votes for Women

Lawmakers were all men. Voters were all men. Most of these men did not want to pass laws giving women the vote. Why not?

- By custom, women did not participate in public affairs. Voting and lawmaking were what men did. Taking care of families was what women did. Many men—and women, too—did not want to change the roles of men and women. They feared that disorder would result.

Breaking the Law

Susan B. Anthony managed to cast her vote in the 1872 presidential election. She was arrested for unlawful voting. She refused to pay the fine of $100, hoping to draw attention to the cause. This cartoon makes fun of her effort.

- Many people believed that suffragists were trouble-makers who put strange ideas into women's heads.

- Many people believed that women were not used to thinking about government and other big ideas. Women would not be able to make smart voting decisions, like men.

Cartoons published at the time showed the viewpoints of many people. These people thought that women's suffrage would lead to an upside-down world. In this world, women wore men's clothing. They gave orders while men did the washing and babysitting.

In this cartoon, a woman leaves her husband with the children while she goes to vote.

CHAPTER 4

Western Voices

Suffragists had two ways to win voting rights. One way was to try to change the U.S. Constitution. In 1878, a senator from California introduced an amendment to the Constitution. It said that the United States government could not deny women the right to vote.

Congress did not take action to get the amendment approved. In the years ahead, suffragists would try again and again to get the bill passed.

The second way to win the vote was state by state. Each state would have to pass laws giving equal voting rights to men and women.

In 1869, lawmakers in Wyoming passed a bill to allow women to vote. The governor signed it into law. At that time, Wyoming was not a state. It was still a territory, with only about 9,000 settlers. Out West, the work of the settlers was hard. Women often worked alongside men, plowing the fields and raising cattle. Perhaps this made it easier for Wyoming to count women and men as equals. Suffragists throughout the nation pointed to Wyoming's decision to give women the vote and said, "It can be done!"

The illustration below shows women voting in Wyoming.

Wyoming was the first territory/state to extend suffrage to women. It was also the first state in which women could serve on a jury (1870) and the first state to elect a female governor (1924).

Wyoming applied to become a state in 1889. Some lawmakers in Congress opposed statehood for Wyoming because women voted there. After a delay, Wyoming became the forty-fourth state in 1890. Its state motto is Equal Rights.

In 1893, suffragists in Colorado persuaded lawmakers to put equal suffrage on the ballot. That meant voters could decide whether women should vote in their state. The voters—all men—said yes. Colorado became the second state in which women could vote.

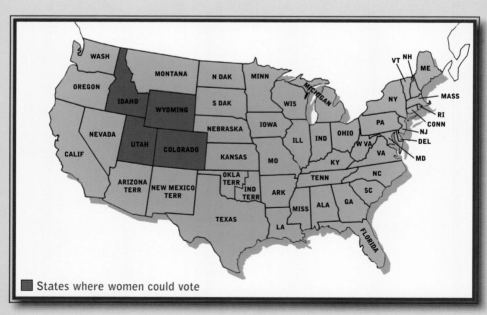

States where women could vote

By 1896, women could vote in only four states.

The third state to approve equal suffrage was Utah, in 1895. In 1896, voters in Idaho approved a ballot item giving women the vote.

Suffragists tried to get equal voting rights in other states. They faced defeat after defeat. At the start of the twentieth century, only four states allowed women to vote. They were all in the West.

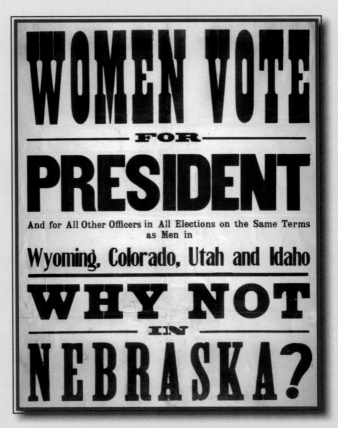

Women in other states soon joined in the effort to gain suffrage.

CHAPTER 5

Protests and Prison

In the early 1900s, the state-by-state plan for women's voting rights was not making much progress. Repeated tries for a suffrage amendment had failed.

Elizabeth Cady Stanton died in 1902. Susan B. Anthony knew that she, too, would not live to see women voting in all the states. She gave a speech shortly before her death in 1906. She urged women to keep fighting. "Failure is impossible," she said.

Younger women took over the national suffrage movement. They decided to focus on changing the Constitution. They demanded a new amendment—the Susan B. Anthony Amendment.

One of the new leaders was Alice Paul. She organized a parade in 1913. Nobody had ever seen anything like it.

The parade took place in Washington, D.C. Eight thousand suffragists came from all over the nation. Led by a young woman on a white horse, they marched toward the White House. Bands played. Banners waved. The mood was proud and festive. A huge crowd watched. Then things turned ugly.

"Go home to your husbands!" men yelled angrily. They began hitting and pushing the marchers. Crowds blocked the street. The police did nothing. Then soldiers arrived to break up the mob. The marchers reached the White House at last.

Women's suffrage parade, Washington, D.C., 1913

Inez Mulholland leads the parade.

Alice Paul (1885–1977) believed that women needed to put on big shows and make a lot of noise to draw attention to their cause. Many suffragists agreed with her. She inspired women to hold demonstrations, parades, and hunger strikes.

Paul had learned her methods in England. She had gone there to study and had joined England's suffrage movement. The suffragists in England held marches and rallies. They were often arrested. Paul had spent time in jail. When she returned to the United States, she was ready to fight for change in bold ways.

Alice Paul believed that the parade had been a big success. Women had stood tall. They had shown strength and firmness. All over the nation, people were reading news reports about the event. Everyone was talking about voting rights and new opportunities for women.

In the early twentieth century, young women had more opportunities than had been available to their mothers or grandmothers. Women attended college. Some became doctors and lawyers. Alice Paul had a PhD in social work.

A woman named Nora Blatch became the first female civil engineer in the nation. She was the granddaughter of Elizabeth Cady Stanton.

NORA STANTON BLATCH,
Now Mrs. Lee de Forest. She is a granddaughter of Elizabeth Cady Stanton, and an expert in wireless telegraphy and
woman suffrage

Pickets

Suffragists wanted President Woodrow Wilson to support their cause. They knew that he could persuade lawmakers to pass the Anthony Amendment. Several suffragists met with President Wilson. But he did not think that women's suffrage was an important goal. "You can afford a little while to wait," he said.

Alice Paul had a new plan—pickets. In January of 1917, women formed a picket line in front of the White House. They held banners and stood in silent protest.

The suffragists picketing the White House were called the "Silent Sentinels."

Day after day, month after month, women took turns on the picket line. "Mr. President, how long must women wait for liberty," read one banner.

Crowds gathered to watch the picketers. Men sometimes tore banners from the women's hands. Then the police began arresting the picketers. Their crime? "Causing a crowd to gather and thus obstructing traffic." The women refused to pay a fine. They were sent to jail.

A mob gathers to watch the picketers.

Action in Washington, D.C.

Women continued to picket. People who were against suffrage attacked them. Police arrested more protesters. Judges' sentences grew harsher. Prison guards treated the women roughly.

Alice Paul was arrested. In jail, she refused to eat. Refusing food is a kind of protest called a hunger strike. Other jailed suffragists began hunger strikes, too. They were force-fed. When a woman refused to open her mouth, she was fed through a feeding tube. Force-feeding was extremely painful.

News reports told of the cruel treatment of the jailed women. Many people believed that the arrests were not lawful. Why were women punished for holding peaceful protests?

President Wilson took action. He pardoned the suffragists, and they were released from jail.

Late in 1917, President Wilson finally took a stand on women's suffrage. He urged Congress to support an amendment giving women the right to vote.

Lawmakers in the House of Representatives passed the amendment. But lawmakers in the Senate voted against it. There were more protests, more jailings, and more talks with lawmakers. In 1919, both houses of Congress passed the amendment. Success! But it still needed approval from three-fourths of the states.

President Woodrow Wilson

A suffragist sits in jail.

CHAPTER 6

The Struggle Ends

Suffragists needed thirty-six states to approve the amendment. They went to work. But so did anti-suffrage groups. Each side tried to persuade state lawmakers. By the end of March 1920, suffragists needed only one more state to vote yes. They hoped they could count on Tennessee.

In the summer of 1920, Tennessee lawmakers met with suffragists. They met with anti-suffragists. They listened to pleas and promises from both sides. The Tennessee Senate voted to approve the amendment. The state's House of Representatives got ready to vote next.

Women celebrate a hard-fought victory.

On the night before the House vote, suffragists did not feel hopeful. They knew which lawmakers were with them and which were against. To win, they would need only one more vote. They would need a miracle.

On August 18, members of the House voted. One of them was a young man named Harry Burn. He was on the anti-suffrage side. But, amazingly, he voted to approve the amendment. Why? He had received a letter from his mother. She had urged him to vote yes.

"I knew that a mother's advice is always safest for her boy to follow," he said later.

The Nineteenth Amendment became the law of the land. At last, women had the vote.

The Nineteenth Amendment

Resolved by the Senate and House of Representatives of the United States of America in Congress assembled (two-thirds of each House concurring therein), That the following article is proposed as an amendment to the Constitution, which shall be valid to all intents and purposes as part of the Constitution when ratified by the legislatures of three-fourths of the several States.

"ARTICLE ————.

"The right of citizens of the United States to vote shall not be denied or abridged by the United States or by any State on account of sex.

"Congress shall have power to enforce this article by appropriate legislation."

F. H. Gillett

In 1920, women throughout the nation voted for president for the first time. Among the new voters was an elderly woman named Charlotte Woodward. When Charlotte was nineteen years old, she had attended a meeting in Seneca Falls, New York. She had signed a document supporting a woman's right to vote. She was the only one of the women signers still alive. She had waited seventy-two years to vote. And the wait was finally over.

Women voting in the 1920 presidential election

Glossary

amendment a change or revision to an existing document

anti-slavery against slavery or the ownership of one person by another

ballot a ticket or slip of paper on which voters mark their votes

bill a draft of a proposed law

Congress the branch of the U.S. government that makes laws. Congress is made up of the Senate and the House of Representatives.

constitution a document that lists the basic laws of a nation

convention a meeting at which people discuss a particular issue

debate to discuss a topic, putting forward different and sometimes opposing viewpoints

oppose to resist, to act against

pamphlet a short essay on a subject of current interest

picket a demonstration outside a place of importance, such as a government office

ridicule talk or actions that make fun of someone

suffrage the right to vote, especially in a political election

suffragist a person who believes in extending voting rights, especially to women

Index